Published in 2015 by

Blue Lotus Books

5858 ave du Parc

Montreal, QC H2V 4H3

email: editor@bluelotusbooks.com

Meticulously crafted and edited for the next level of the coloring experience, this book offers a magical mystery tour into the exquisite world of Alfons Maria Mucha. All drawings are lovingly adapted and hand drawn to bring his art and spirit closer to yours, in high fidelity and style. The page layouts are derived from Muha's work, designed to delight and transport you into his reality.

Get inspired by one of the great masters of the 20th century and channel his creative genius through your unique color palette. Raise to the challenge that his intricate drawings may pose or relax into the more forgiving compositions in the book. Delve into a chapter of art history while flexing, relaxing, enhancing your coloring skills. Enjoy!

Da Zain

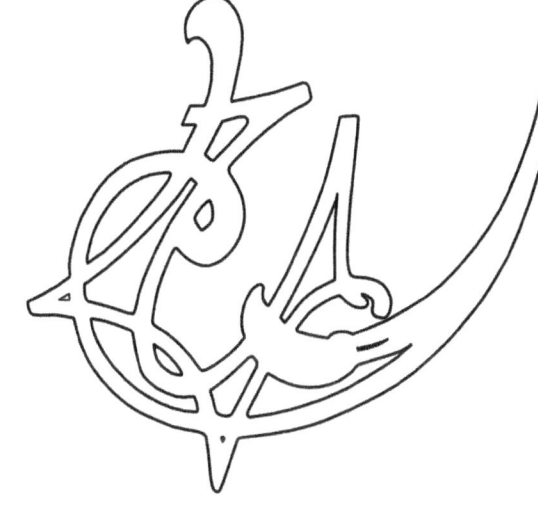

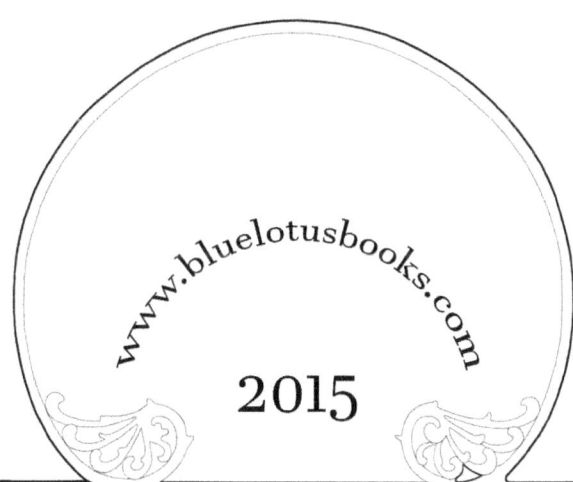

www.bluelotusbooks.com

2015

Art Nouveau

The advent of photography in 19th century precipitated both a crisis and a revolution in the traditional visual arts. The notion of art as mimesis of reality, i.e. as a way to reflect space and capture time, was challenged by the life like fidelity of the photographic image. Artists began to reexamine and redefine art, questioning traditional schools and distancing themselves from the academic approach. Art stepped into modernity, led by a number of movements that broke away from traditional styles in order to pursue progressive avenues for reinventing the form.

Art Nouveau is the French name used to refer to one of those secessionist movements of the early 20th century. The style emerged in several European countries concurrently and was thus known by different names - Secession in Austria-Hungary, Arts and Crafts movement in Britain, Modern in Russia, Jugendstil in Germany, Modernisme in Spain. Inspired by industrial developments, it was using new materials and techniques to re-position art in the new era. Thus it became the first movement to foreground mass produced graphics as opposed to traditional (limited edition) printing techniques, for example. Many of the works included in this book were intended for mass, or at least repetitive, production. In addition, Mucha often reused his designs in full or in part for different projects, often applying more than one color palette to the same image. This is also one of the reasons why his work is so well suited for coloring book adaptation – by coloring Mucha's drawings, the colorist co-produces and perpetuates Mucha's art in congruence with the artist's own practice.

Mucha was not thrilled with the popularity he gained through his commercial art as he believed art's purpose was to channel messages of the spirit. This is why colouring this drawings as a way to meditation would be the best homage the colourist could pay to this remarkable artist.

The preoccupation of Art Nouveau with the problems and possibilities of industrialization generated a focus on design. This was apparent in Mucha's work where his signature drawing line was as adaptable to painting as it was transferable to print and commercial design. Images from his commercial projects recur in his paintings, suggesting how he used one medium as research ground for another. The boundaries between fine and applied arts were blurred, the original became mass (re)producible and vice versa. This comprehensive applicability of Art Nouveau across the borders of visual and material arts was one of the major characteristic of the style. The design of this book pays homage to the way Art Nouveau permeated every facet of material culture – each page is conceived and framed as a visual piece, as an object of design as art.

Alfons Mucha was a pioneer of the style, introducing his vision to the Parisian public through an original series of posters he produced for Sarah Bernhardt that put him on the Parisian art map. His influence became so powerful that before the term Art Nouveau was coined in France, the style was referred to as Mucha Style.

Alfons Maria Mucha (1869-1939)

Alfons Maria Mucha (a.k.a Alphonse Maria Mucha) was born in 1869 in the town of Ivancice, Moravia (then in Austria-Hungary and currently in the Czech Republic). He received his secondary education in Moravia, then worked as theater stage designer, mural painter and decorative artist in Moravia and Vienna, before joining the Munich Academy of Art. There he became part of a group of Slavic students/artists which marked the beginning of his commitment to a Pan-Slavic artistic ideal. In 1897, Mucha moved to Paris to continue his academic studies and pursue his art. He was working mainly as an illustrator for magazines and advertisers when in 1895 was hired to make a poster for a Sarah Bernardt show. This landed him a 6 year contract with the actress, and a contract with Champenois, one of the leading printers of the period. He became a household name around the world.   As a leading Art Nouveau artist, Mucha produced a significant body of work in painting, printmaking, and object design in Europe, North America and the Middle East, but his dreaming heart was set on a major series of large paintings called the *Slavic Epic*. After securing the financial support of American Charles Richard Crane, he returned to his motherland to realize the project which took him close to 18 years to complete. In 1918, after the dissolution of Austria-Hungary at the end of World War I, and the consolidation of Czechoslovakia, Mucha's designs appeared on the first Czechoslovakian postage stamps. The following year they appeared on the national bank notes. In 1928, Mucha and Charles Richard Crane presented the complete

Slavic Epic to the City of Prague to mark the 10th anniversary of the creation of Czechoslovakia.

Mucha's late work focused on large format projects and mural painting. After Hitler's coming to power, Mucha started research for a painting about the horrors of war. In turn, Slavic Nationalism in general and Mucha's work in particular was denounced as reactionary. In 1938 his health began to deteriorate. After the Nazi annexation of Czechoslovakia, Mucha was arrested by Gestapo, but released after several days of questioning. His health continued to deteriorate and he died later that same year of 1939, 10 days before his 79th birthday.

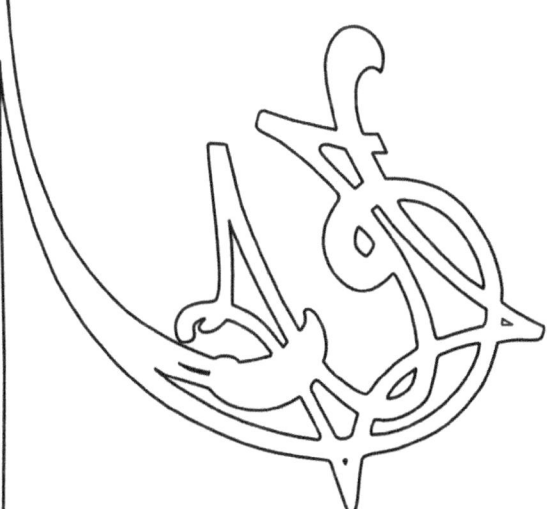

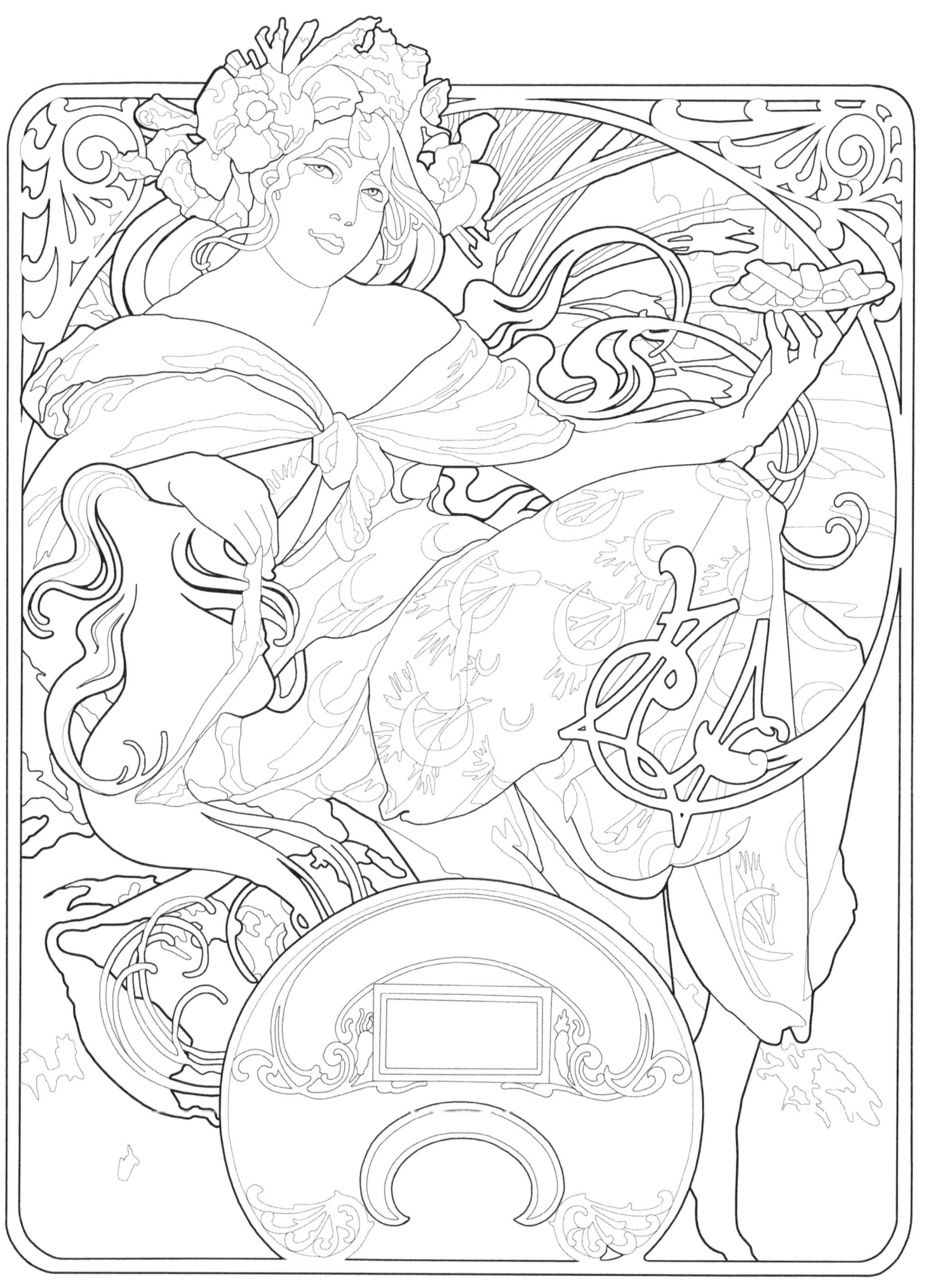

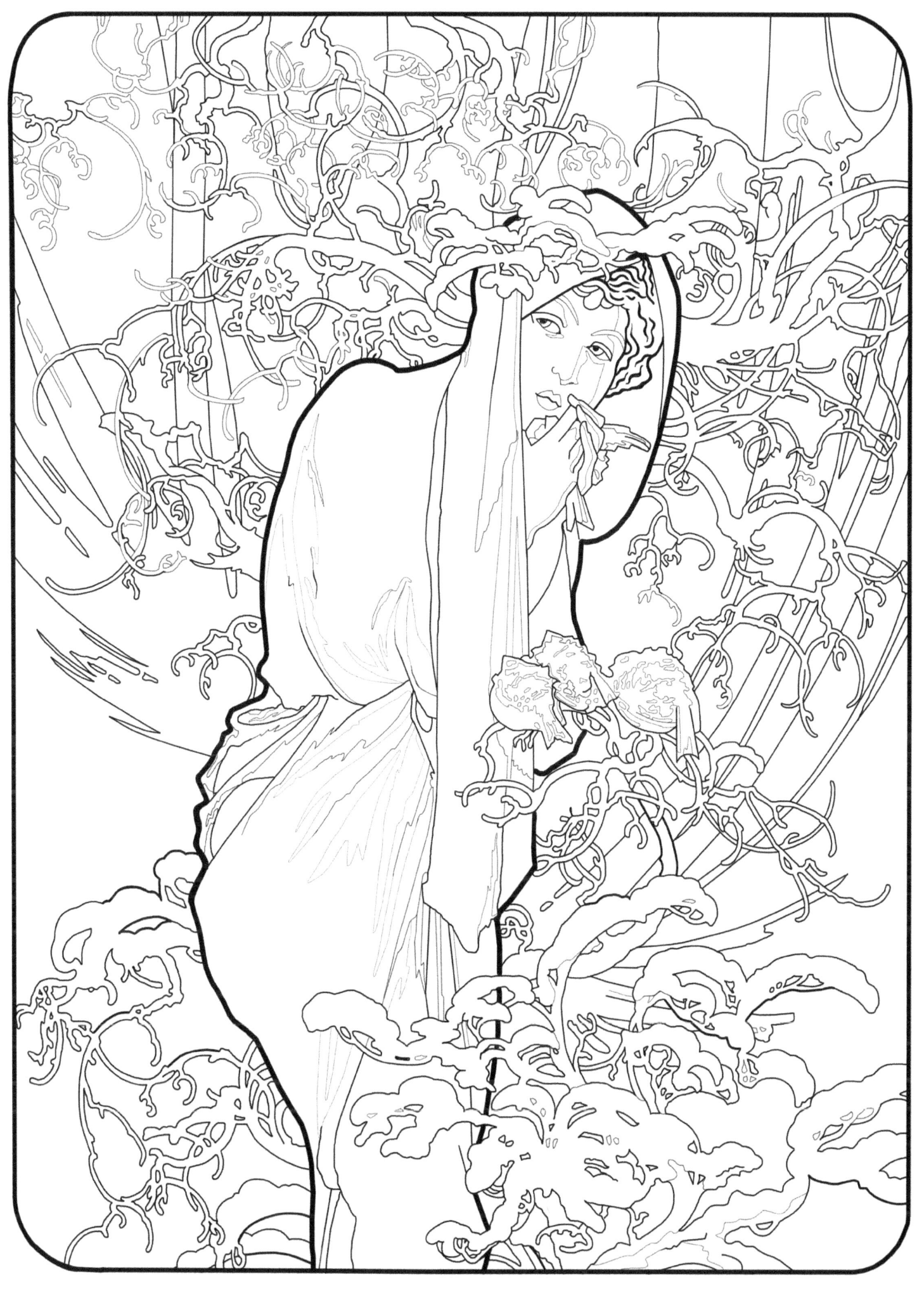

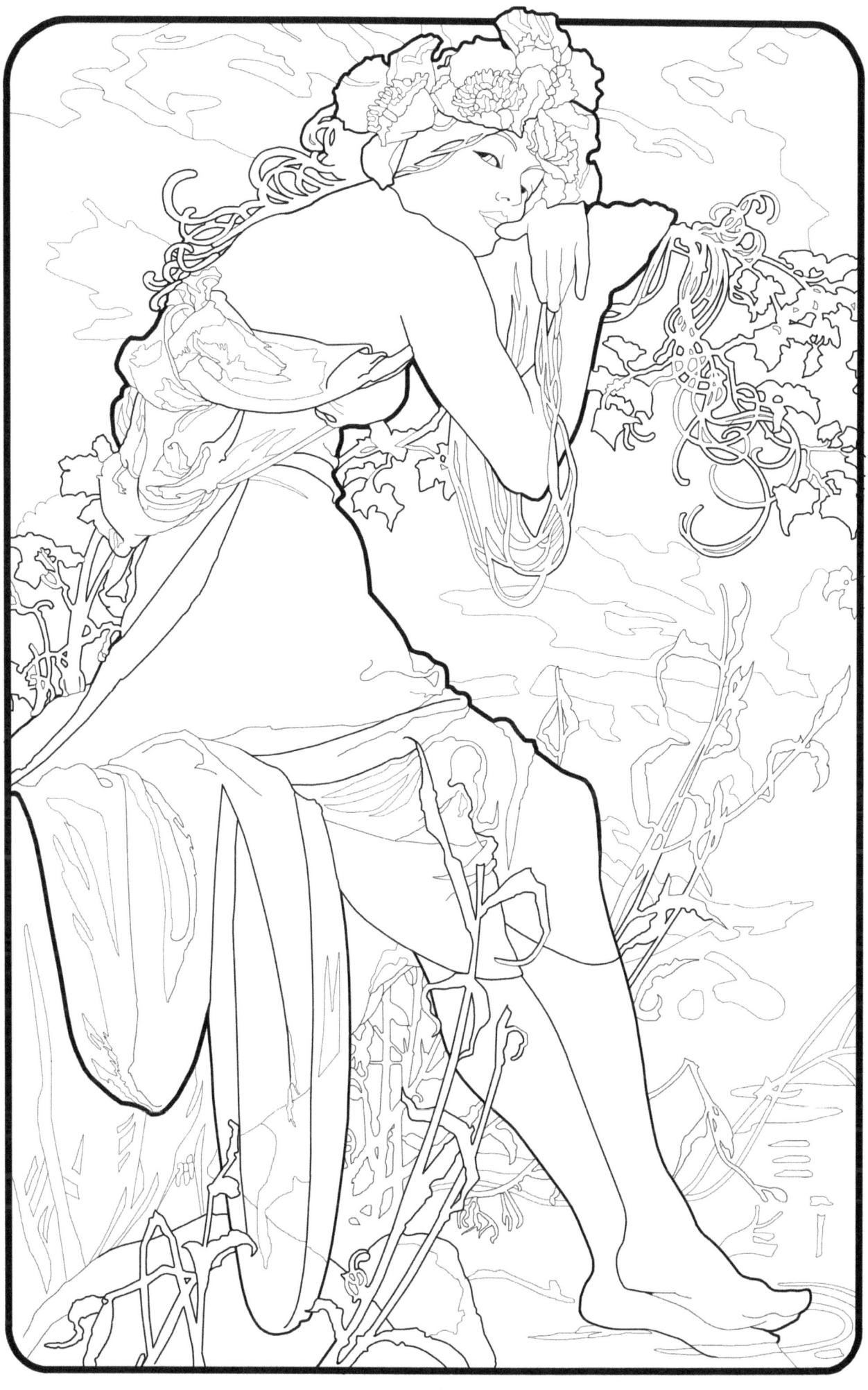

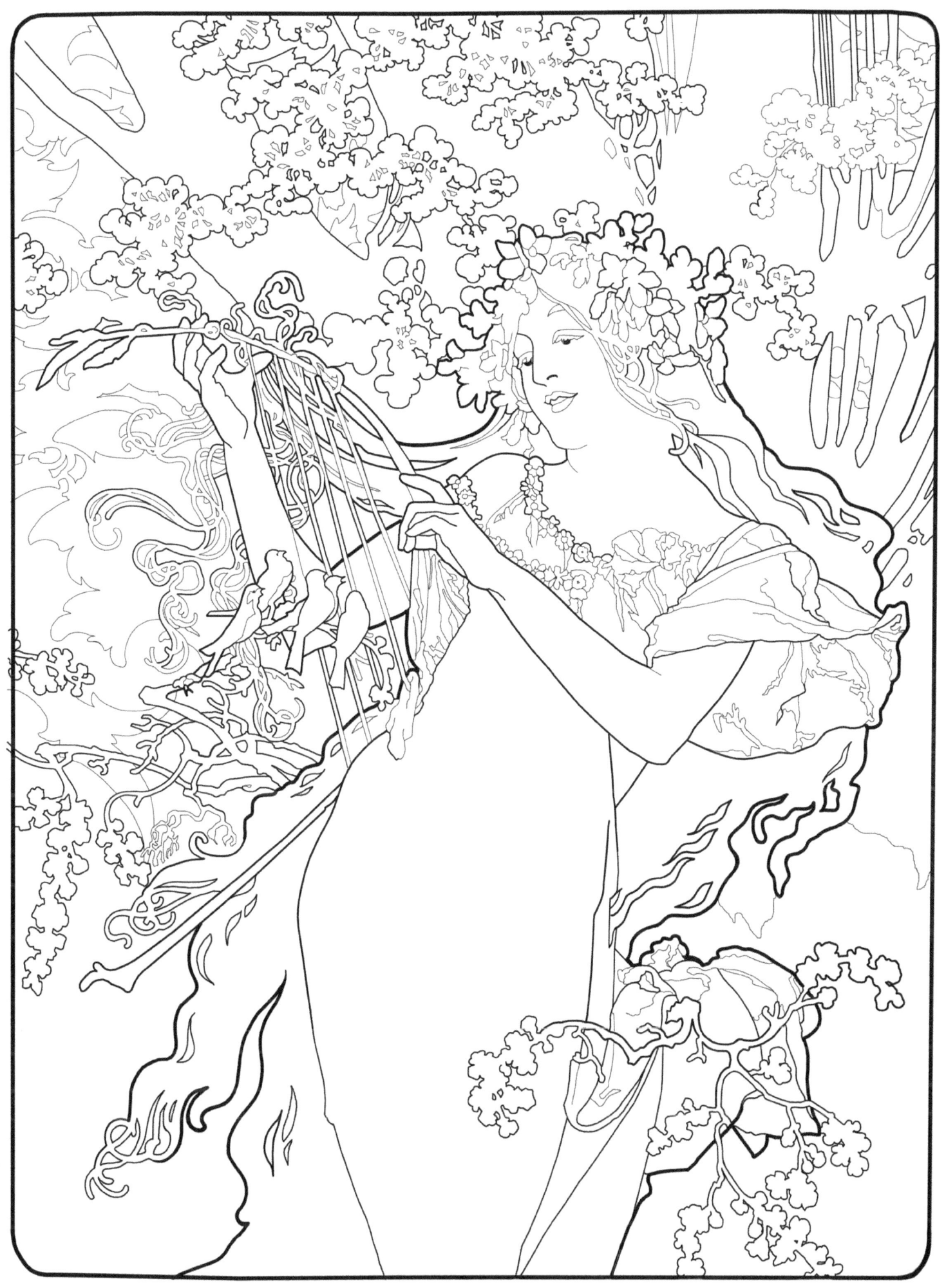

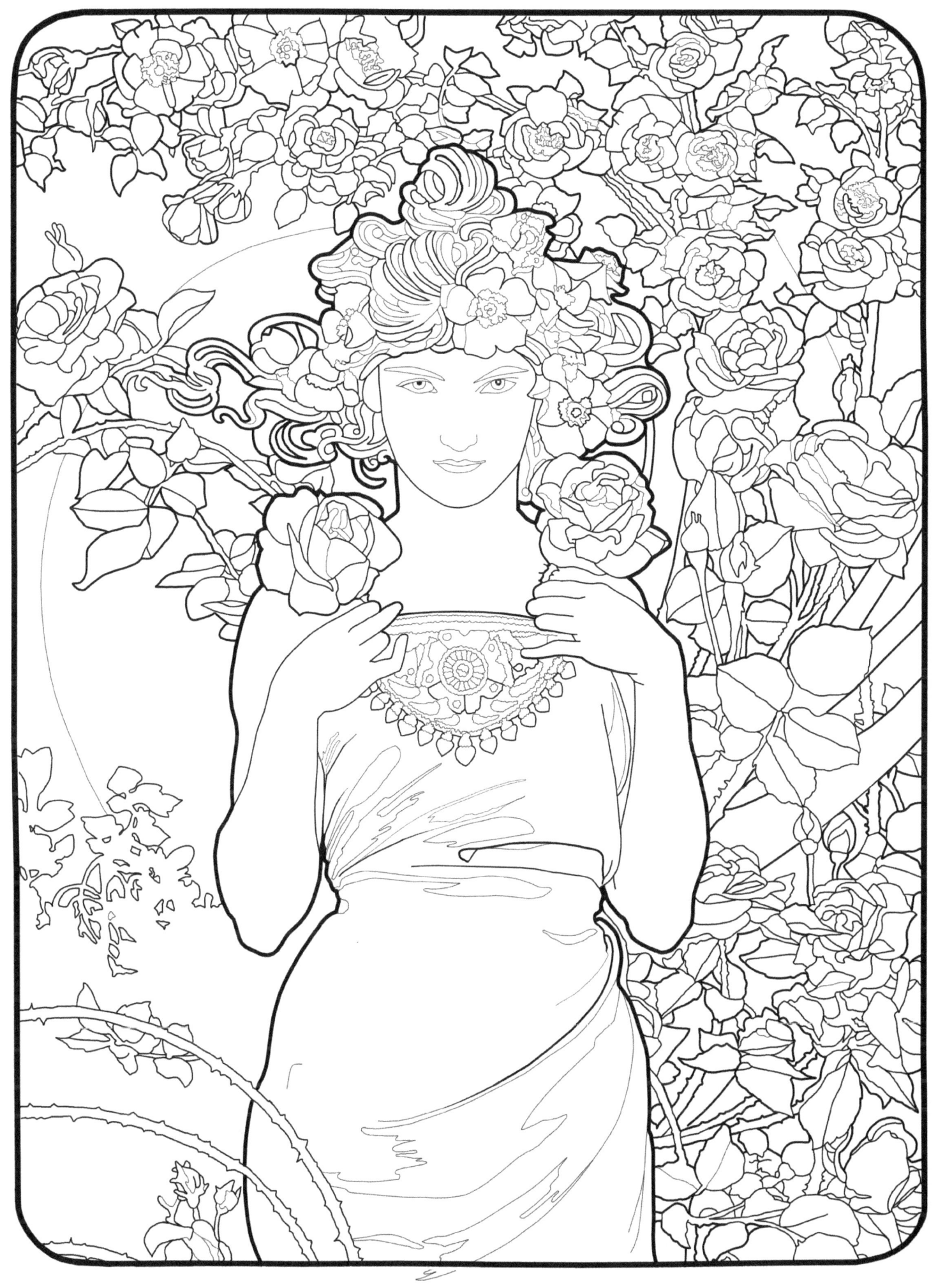

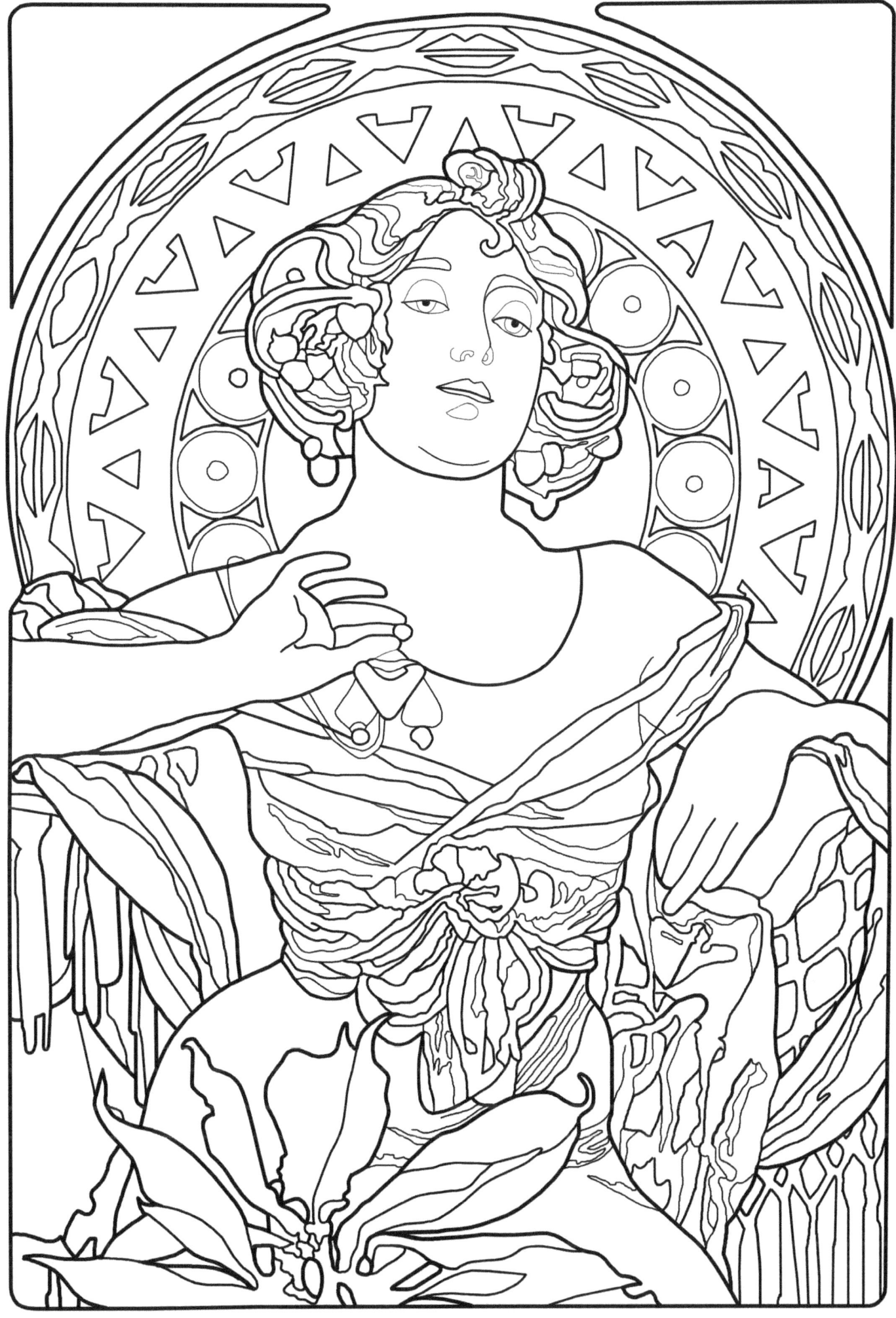

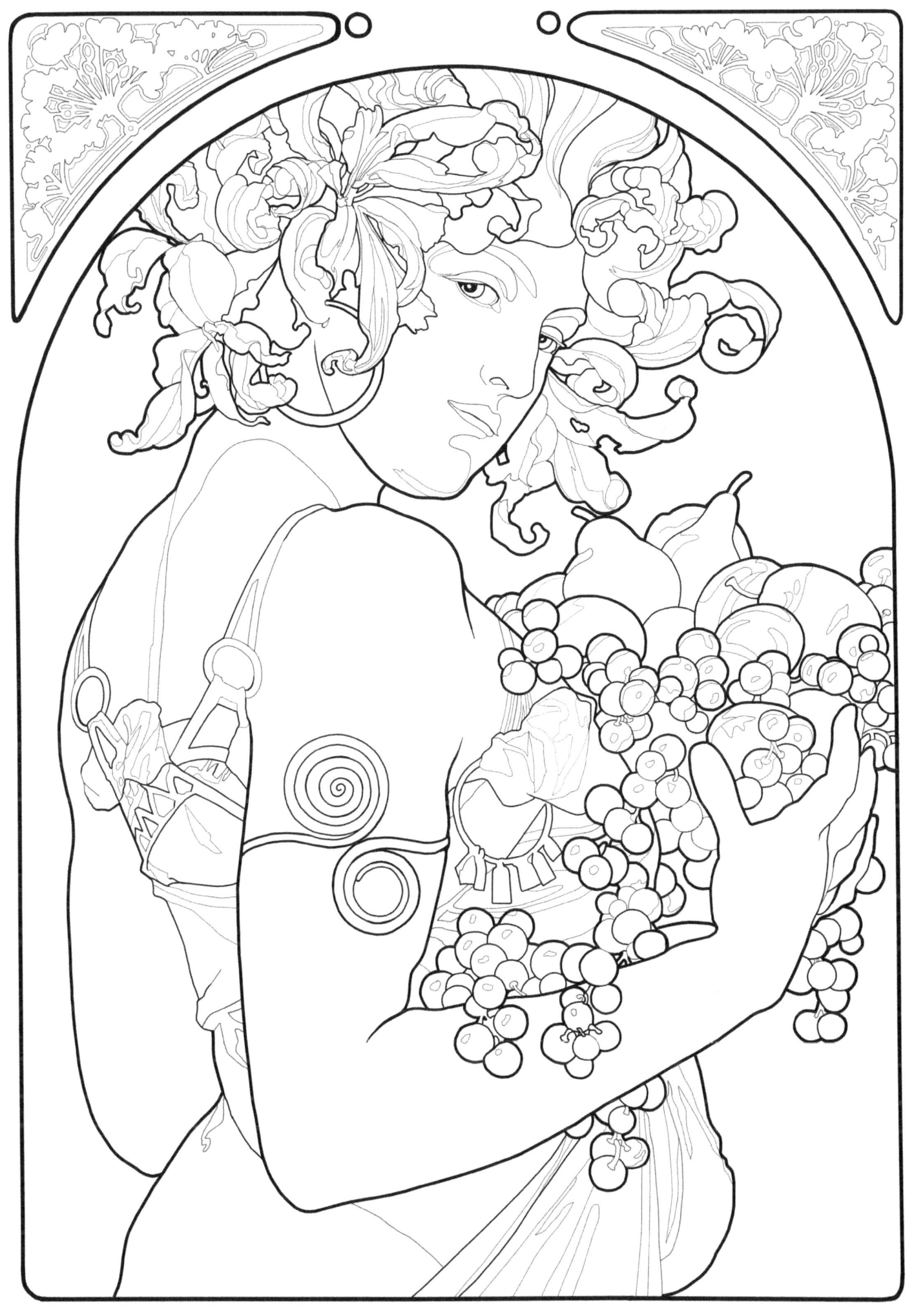

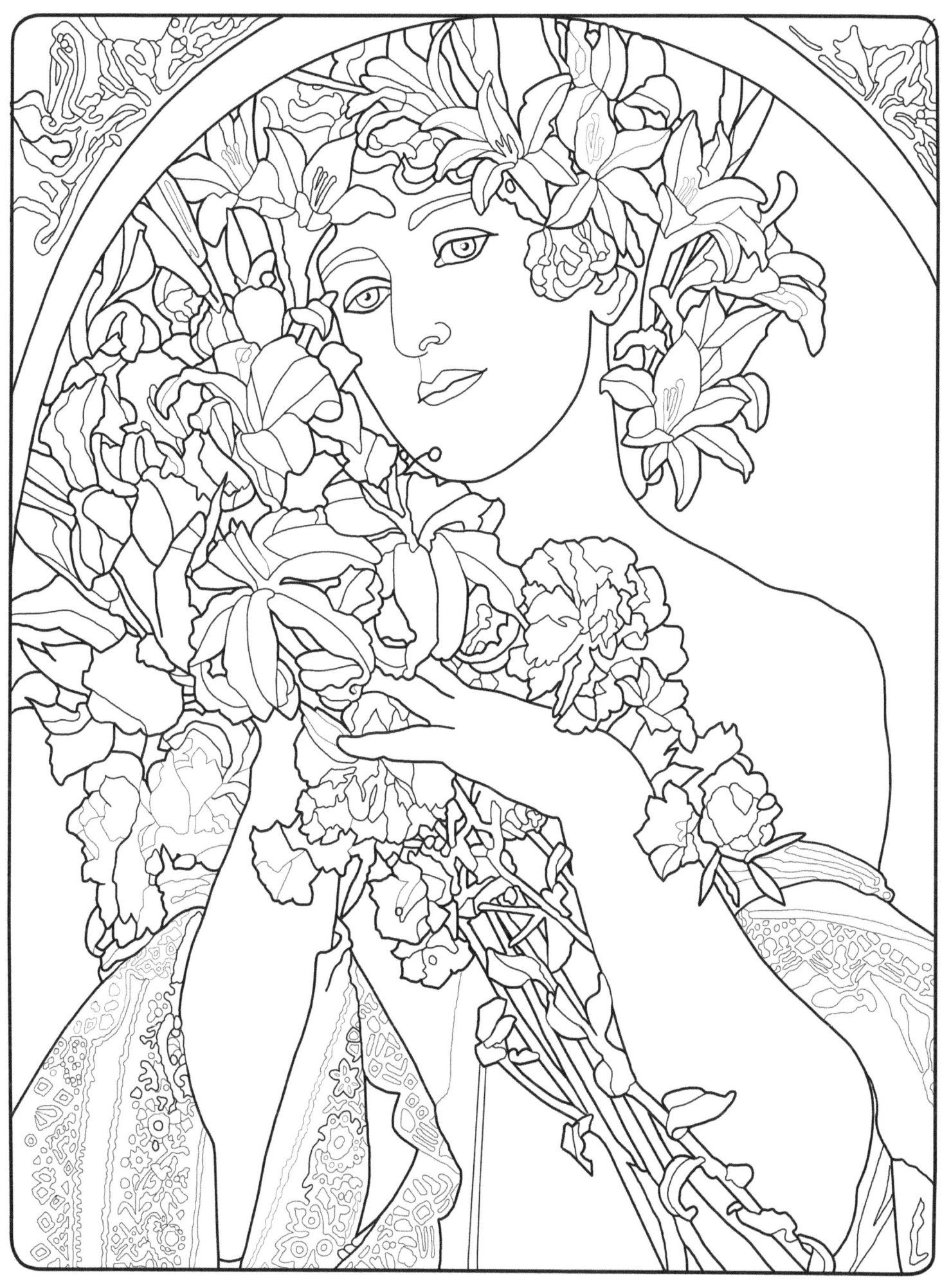

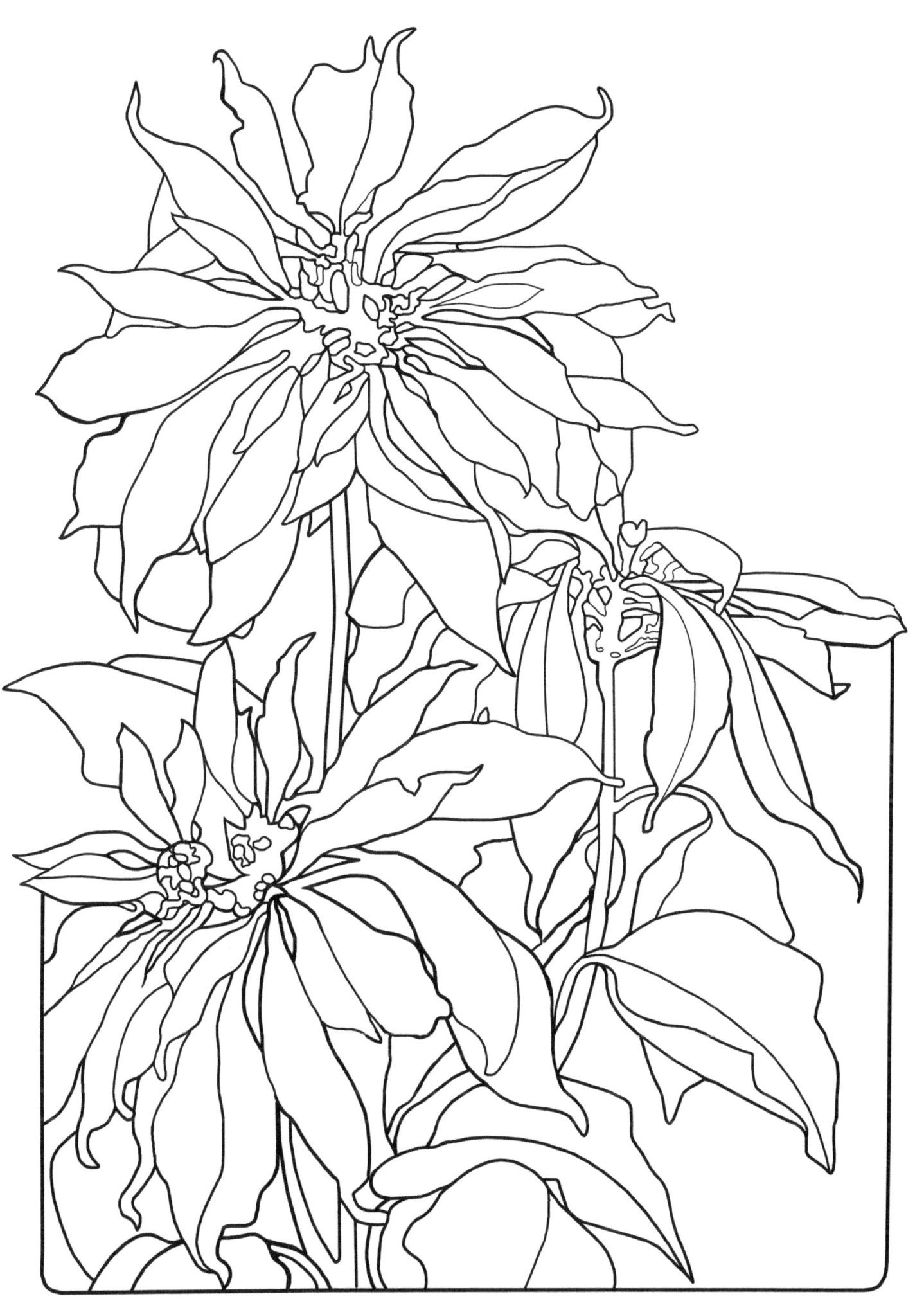

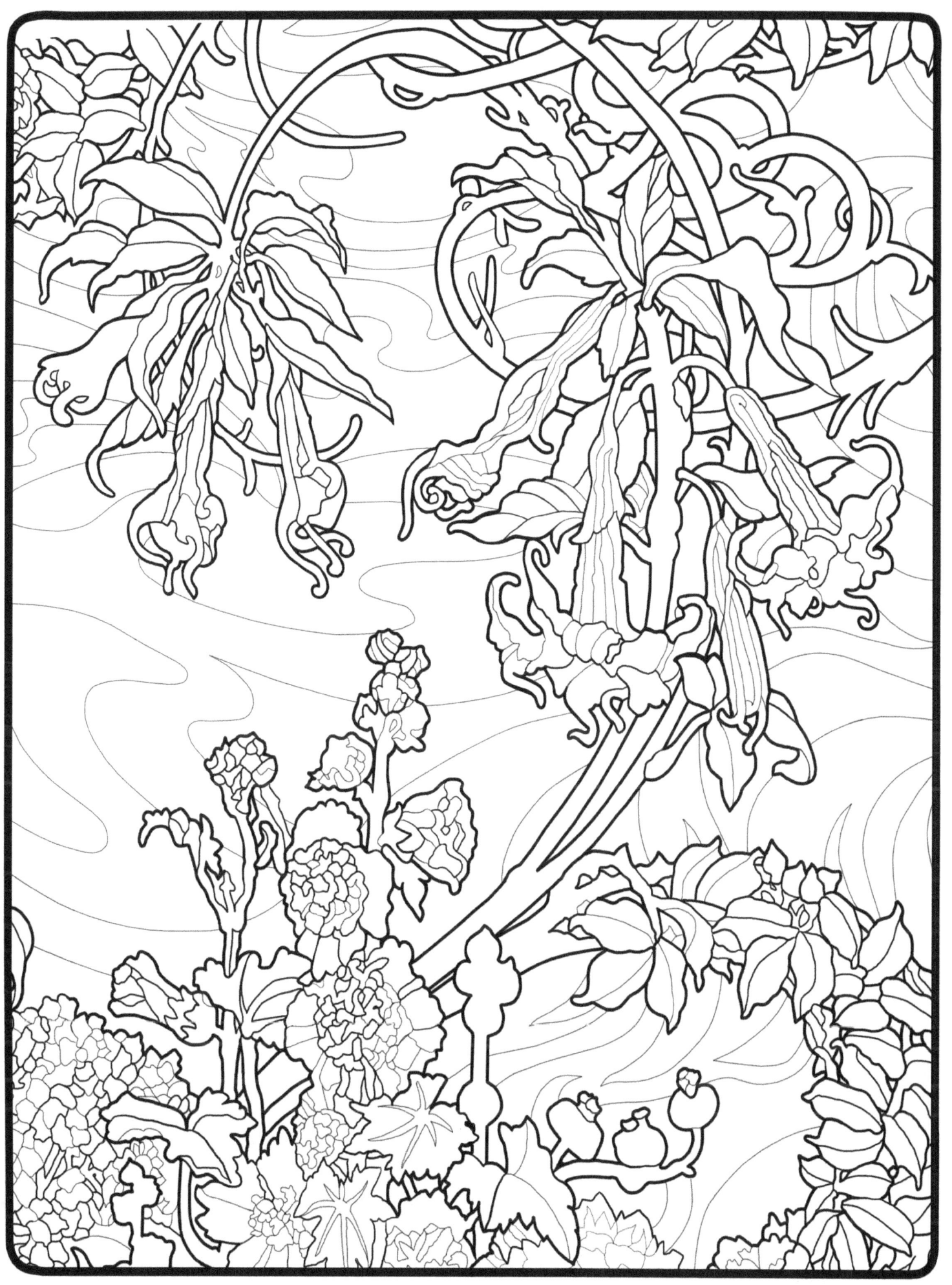

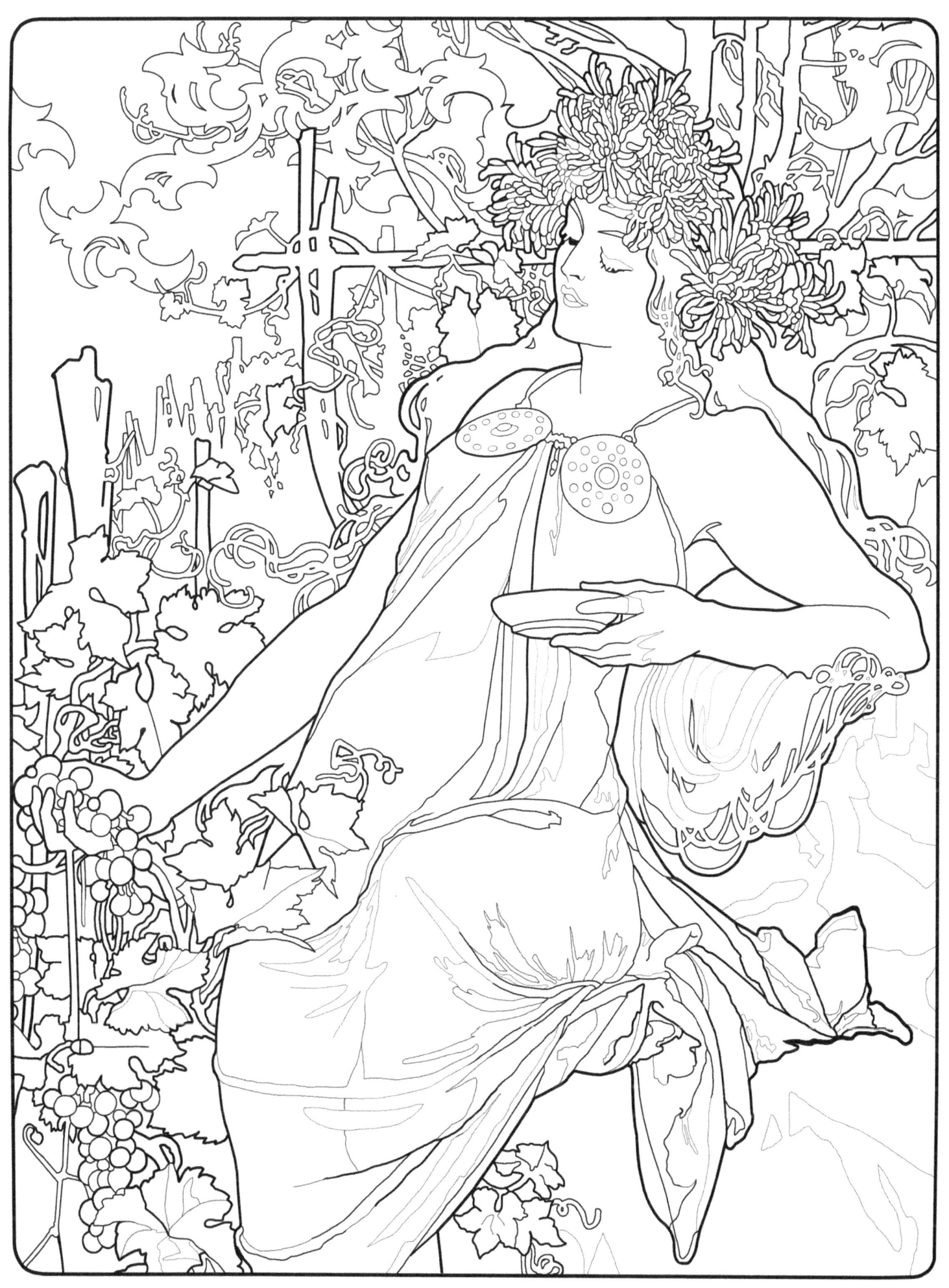

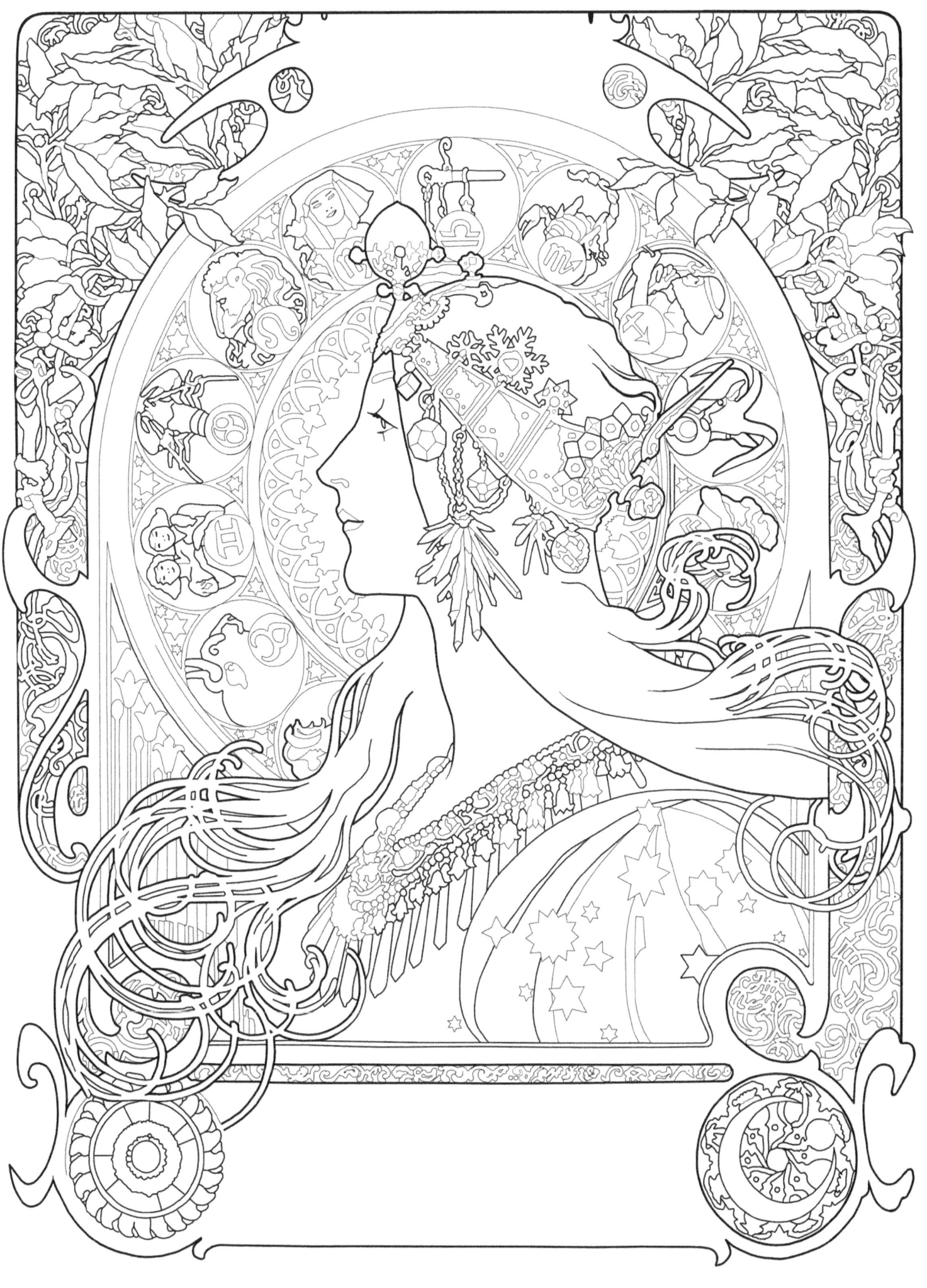

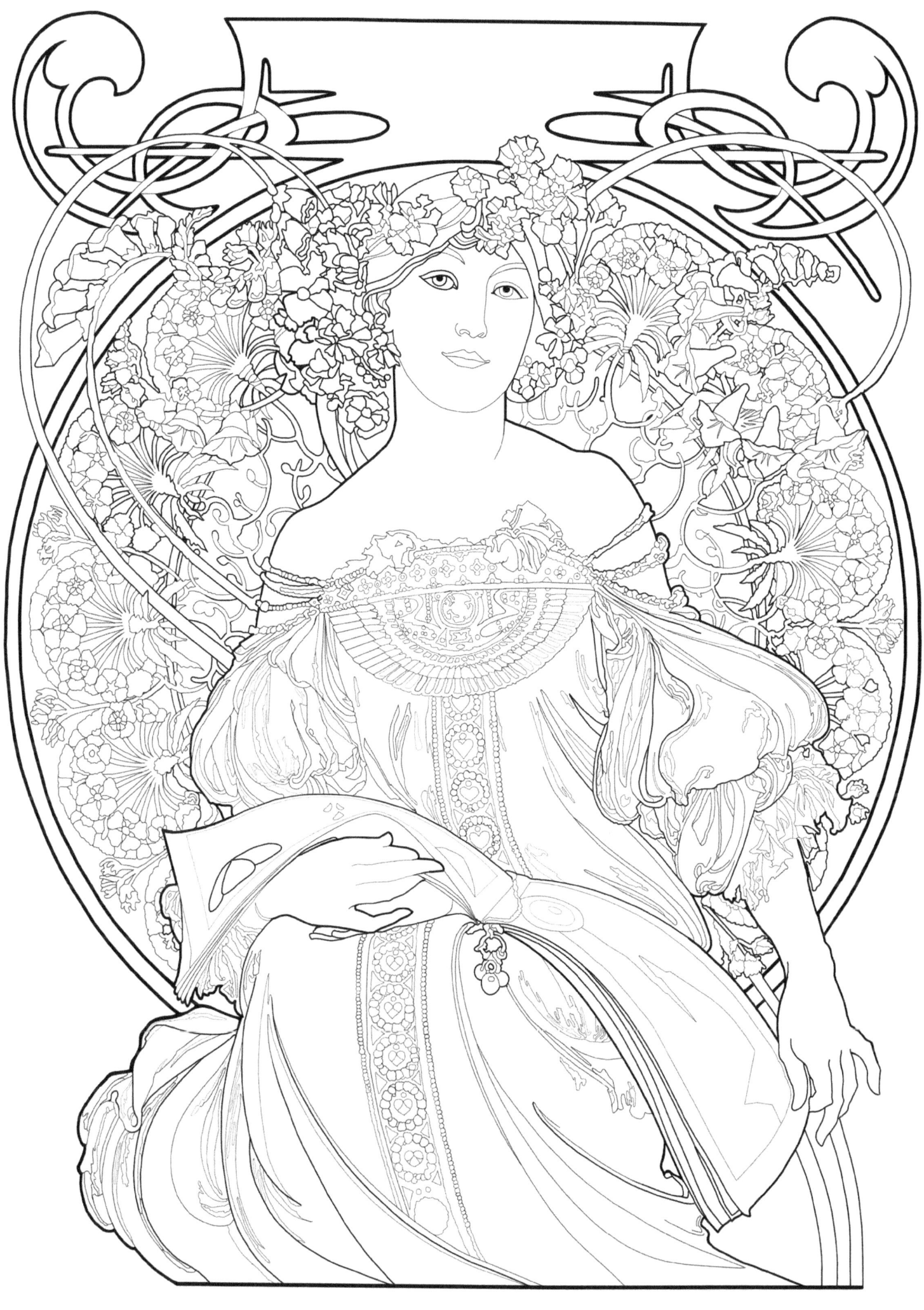

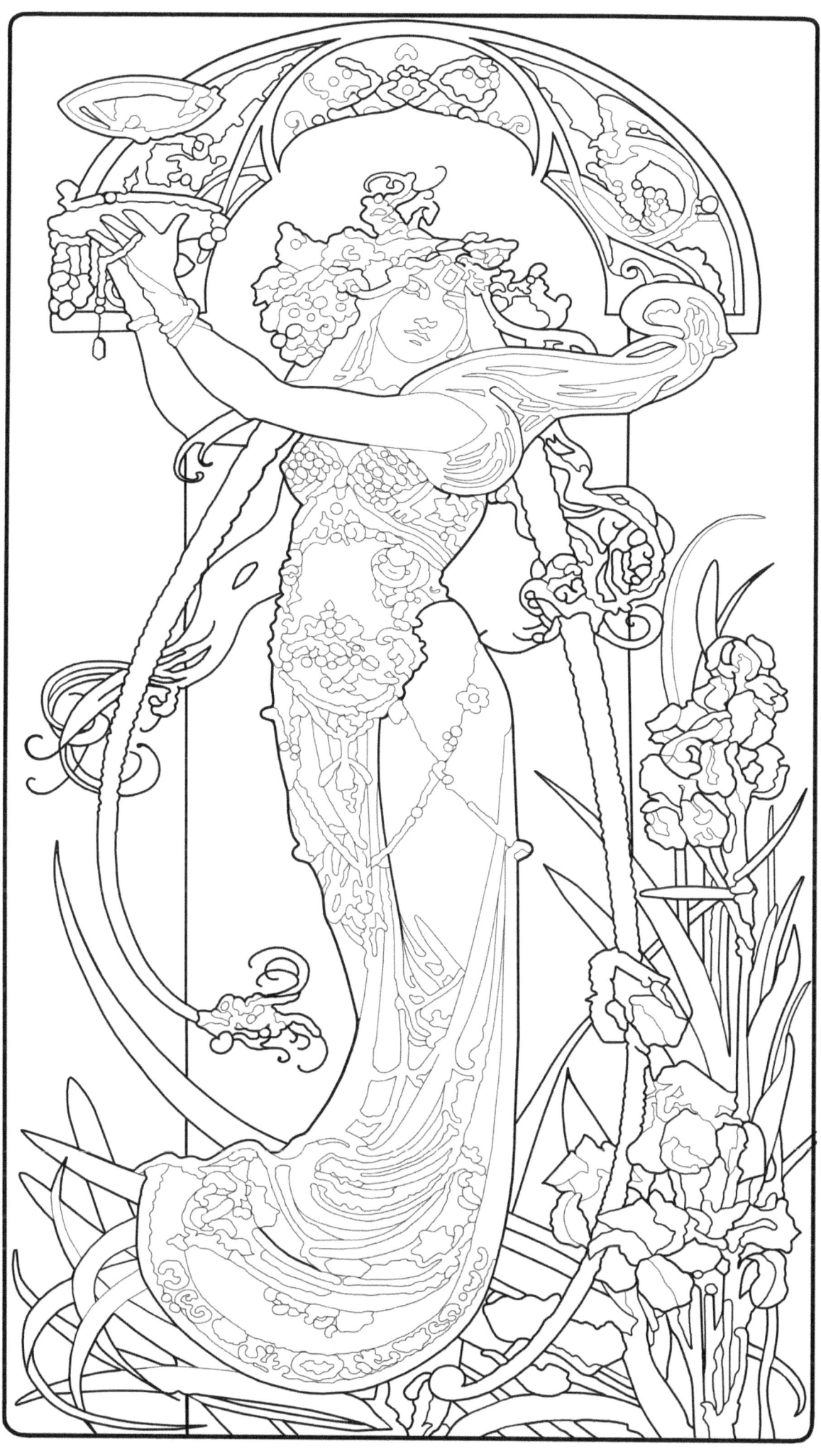

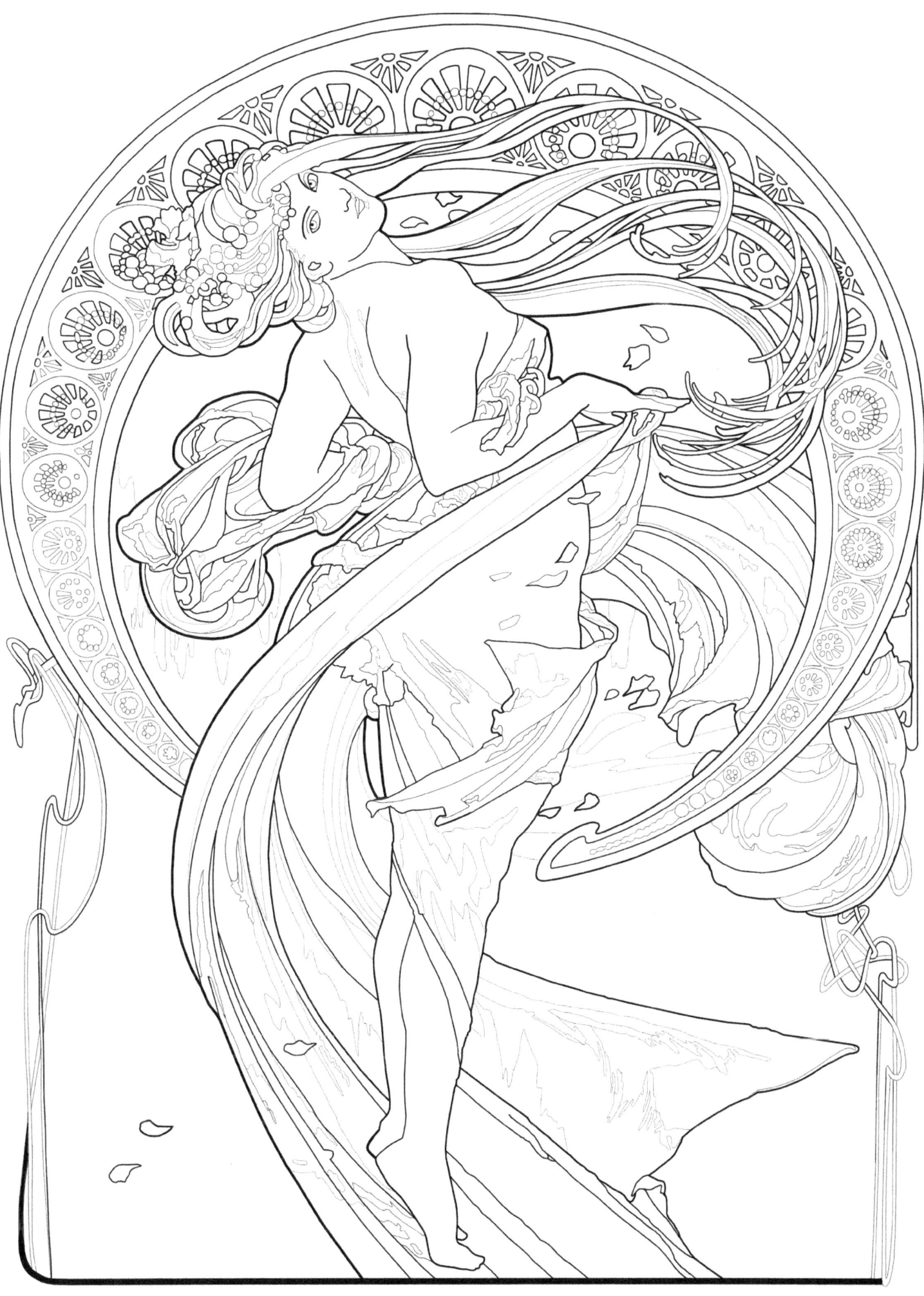

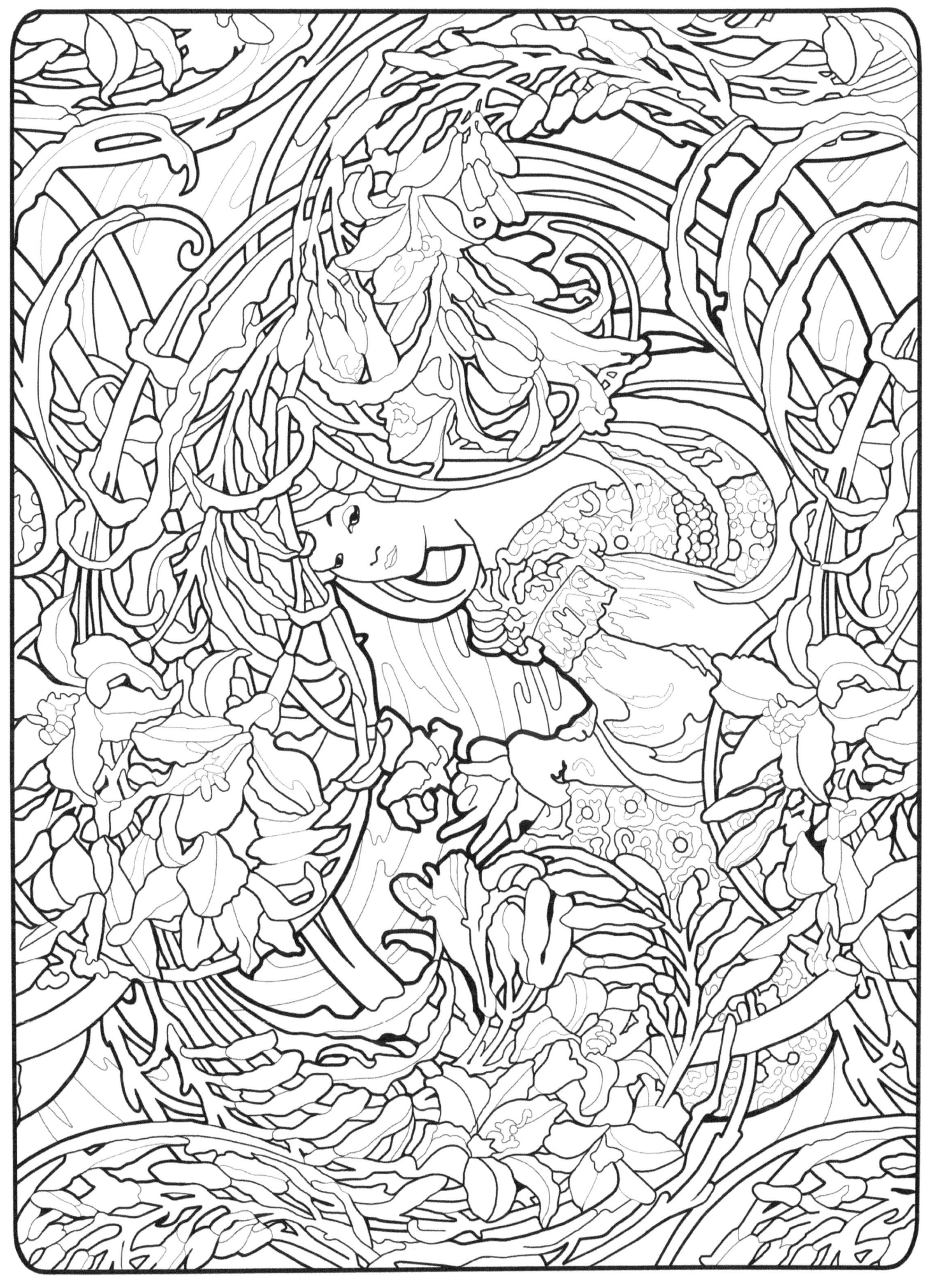

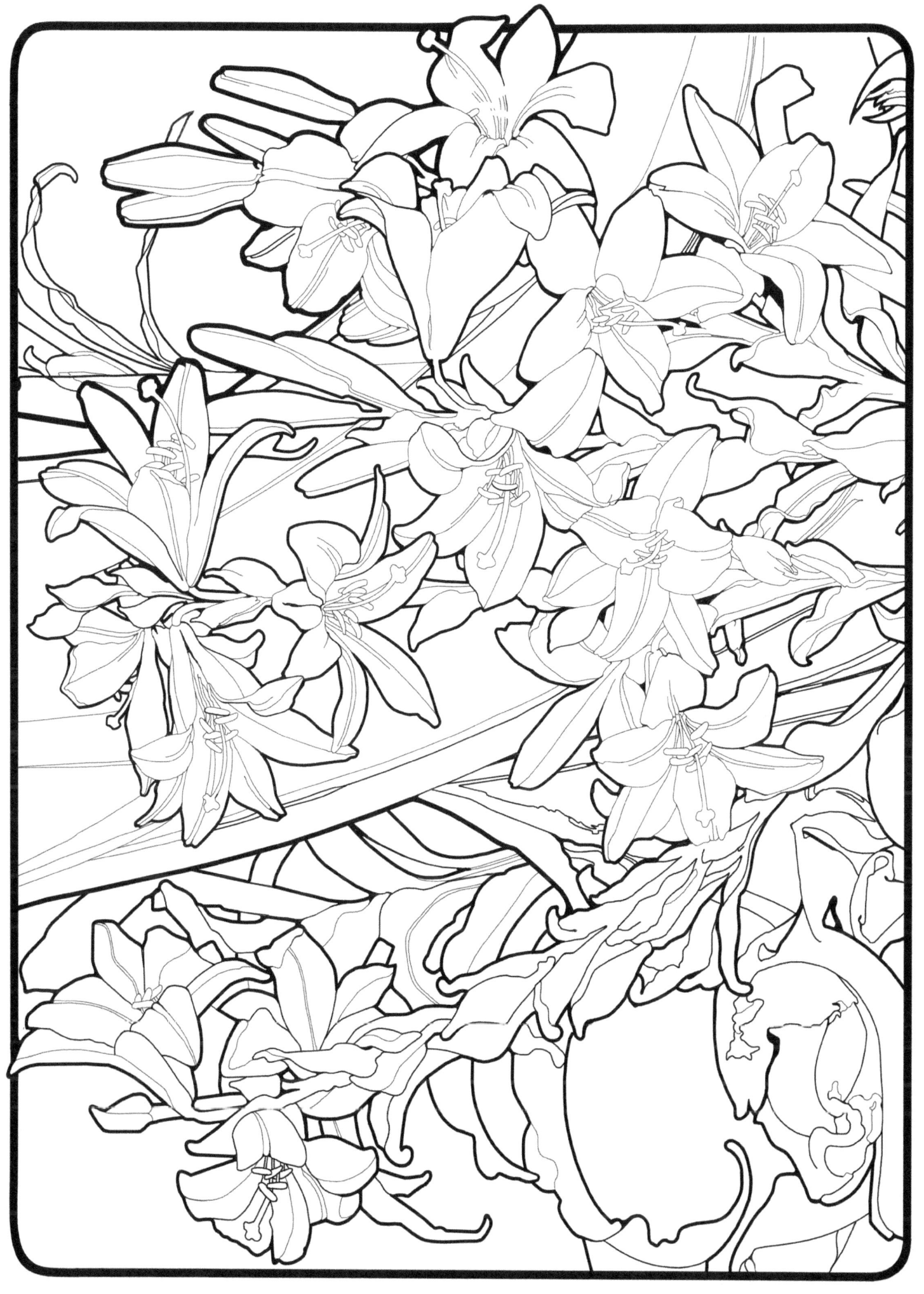

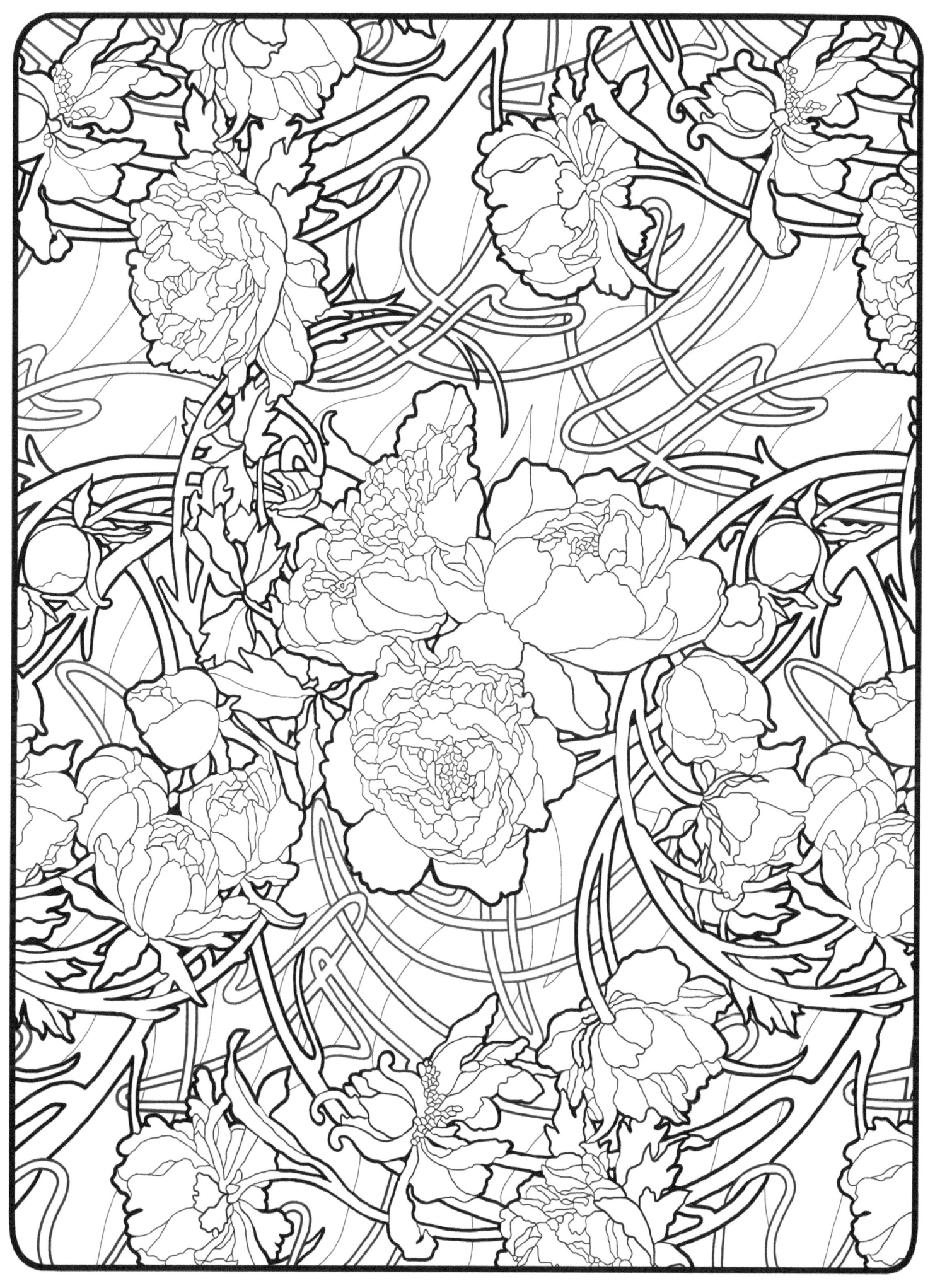

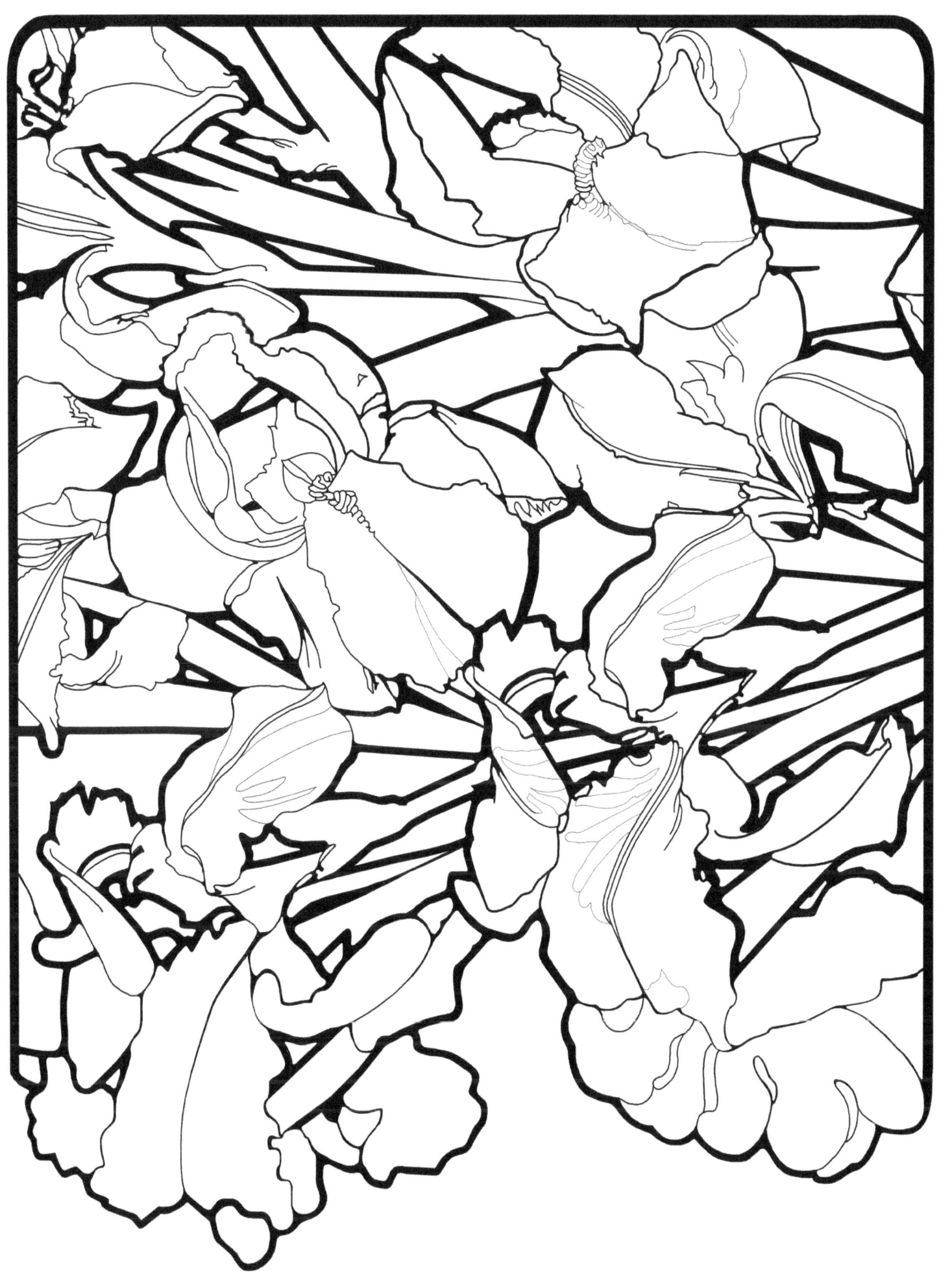

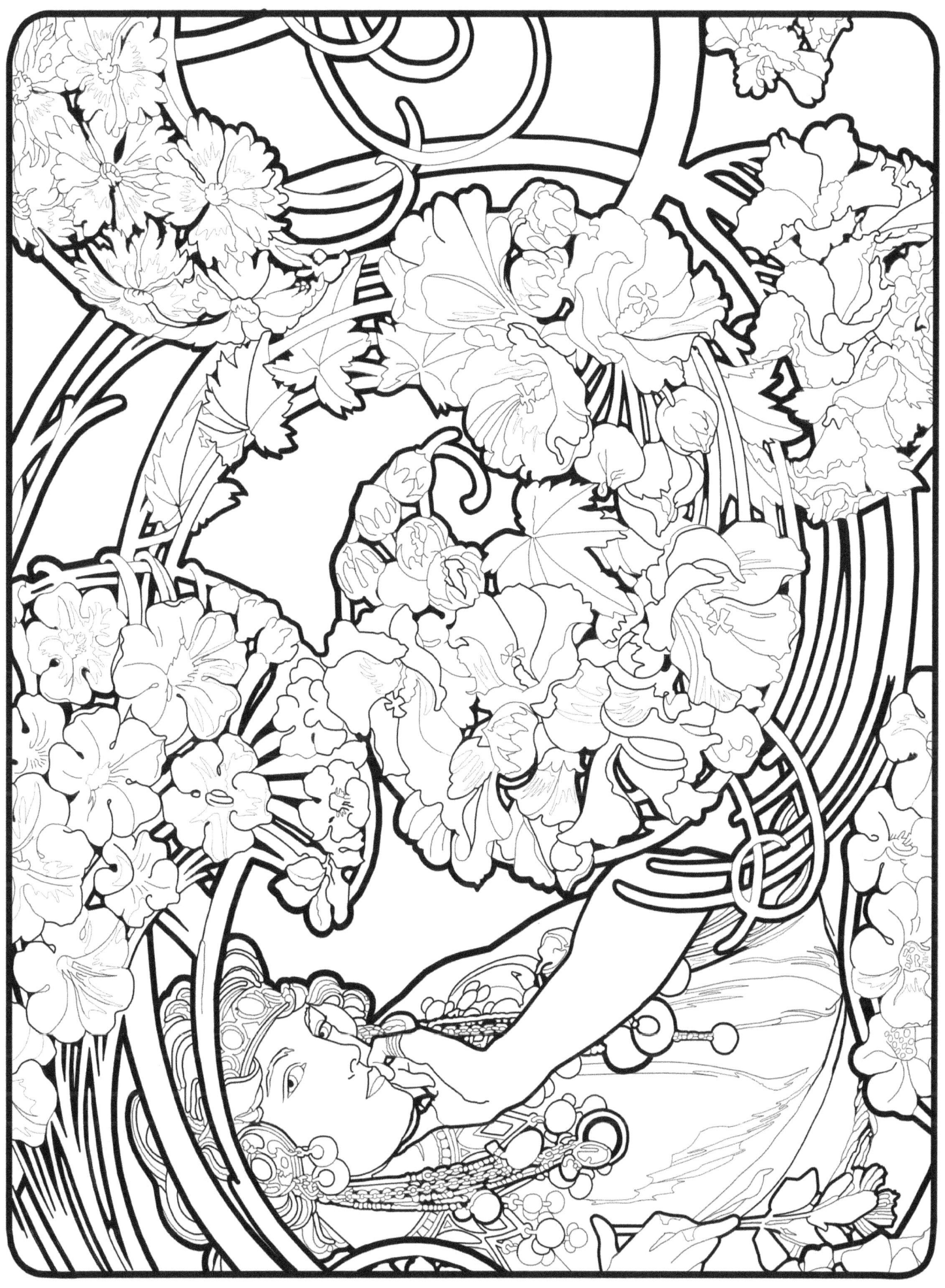

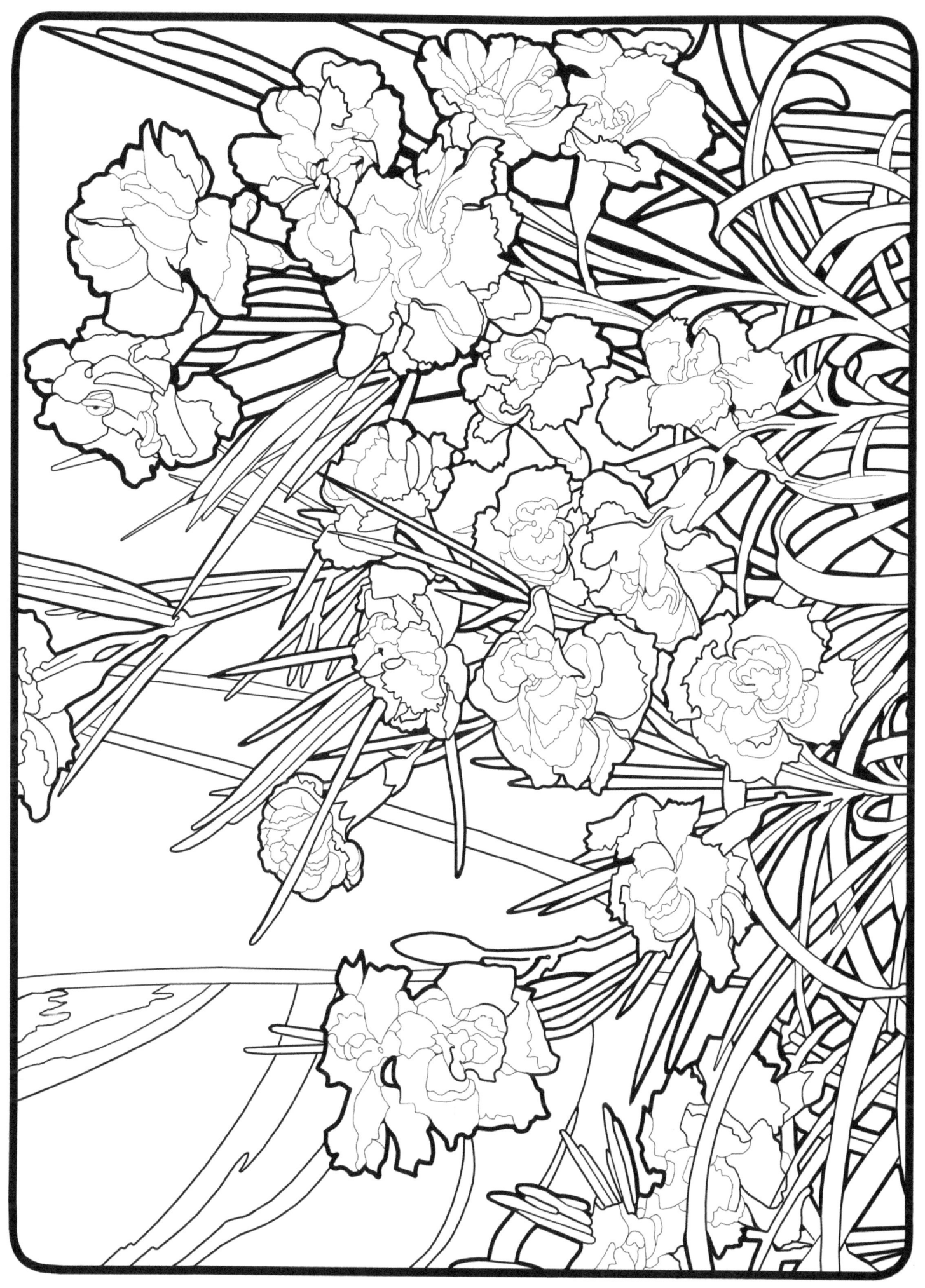

Thank you for buying the paperback version of *Creative Color Inspirations: Alfons Mucha*!

If you enjoyed this book and have a moment to share, please leave us your feedback on our Amazon page.

For special offers and to keep informed about our upcoming books, free sample giveaways and coloring art competitions, join our Facebook page:

https://www.facebook.com/ExquisiteColorBook

After you have practiced on this paperback edition, and you would like to produce high quality versions of your final art work, treat yourself to the deluxe print version which also makes a great gift. You can get it at one of the links below:

Amazon Canada - http://www.amazon.ca/Creative-Colour-Inspirations-Exquisite-Collection/dp/0994982909

Amazon US - http://www.amazon.com/dp/0994982925

For more information about our products, visit our website at http://www.bluelotusbooks.com

www.ingramcontent.com/pod-product-compliance
Lightning Source LLC
Chambersburg PA
CBHW080639190526
45169CB00009B/3436